focus on the family®

Women of
PURPOSE

FOCUS
ON THE
FAMILY®

Gospel Light

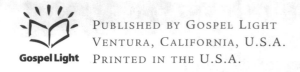

PUBLISHED BY GOSPEL LIGHT
VENTURA, CALIFORNIA, U.S.A.
PRINTED IN THE U.S.A.

Gospel Light is a Christian publisher dedicated to serving the local church. We believe God's vision for Gospel Light is to provide church leaders with biblical, user-friendly materials that will help them evangelize, disciple and minister to children, youth and families.

It is our prayer that this Gospel Light resource will help you discover biblical truth for your own life and help you minister to others. May God richly bless you.

For a free catalog of resources from Gospel Light, please call your Christian supplier or contact us at 1-800-4-GOSPEL *or* www.gospellight.com.

PUBLISHING STAFF
William T. Greig, Chairman · **Dr. Elmer L. Towns,** Senior Consulting Publisher · **Bayard Taylor, M.Div.,** Senior Editor, Biblical and Theological Issues · **Sarah O'Brien,** Contributing Writer

ISBN 0-8307-3701-4
© 2005 Focus on the Family
All rights reserved.
Printed in the U.S.A.

Any omission of credits is unintentional. The publisher requests documentation for future printings.

To protect the privacy of the individuals whose quotations have been used in this book, names have been fictionalized. All quotations are used with permission.

Scripture quotations are taken from the *Holy Bible, New International Version*®. Copyright © 1973, 1978, 1984 by International Bible Society. Used by permission of Zondervan Publishing House. All rights reserved.

contents

Unexpected Detours—Surrendering Our Dreams

One of our greatest challenges is to make a subtle shift in our thinking: *We were made for God's purposes; God was not created for our purposes.* This shift in thinking will enable us to handle the detours of life more gracefully.

God's Call—Understanding Our True Purpose

Life is not about getting from point A to point B so that we can really begin to live. We must focus on the process that takes us from point A to point B, and that process is about knowing God and defining our identity by His.

The Master's Plan—Learning to Yield

We may think that when we accomplish our goals or dreams, then we will know God better and be able to serve or follow Him more fully. But God says our purpose is to bring Him glory in all that we do—whether big or small in our eyes.

Broken Dreams—Waiting for God's Promised Blessings

None of us plans or invites chaos, and yet chaos finds us all at some point. Where is God when chaos arrives? Is He punishing us for something we've done, or might He be doing something else?

WOMEN OF PURPOSE

"For I know the plans I have for you," declares the Lord, "plans to prosper you and not to harm you, plans to give you hope and a future. Then you will call upon me and come and pray to me, and I will listen to you. You will seek me and find me when you seek me with all your heart."

JEREMIAH 29:11-13

Imagine that you have had a lifelong dream to see Yosemite National Park. What if God were to call you and say, "I'd like to be with you this weekend. What would you think about going on a camping trip with Me to Yosemite National Park? I would love to show you Half Dome, Bridalveil Falls and El Capitan." Ecstatic, you agree, and before long the two of you are on your way, enjoying your time together. As you climb higher, the air becomes crisper, full of a pine scent; but although the scenery is pleasant, you don't really notice because you are so anxious to arrive at this spectacular place that you have always dreamt of seeing. You look ahead and notice a tunnel carved into the side of the mountain. As you enter it, you realize that you can't see the other end. You are surrounded by darkness. God assures you that everything will be fine; the most spectacular view is just on the other side of the tunnel. Prone to claustrophobia, you hold your breath—awaiting the promised land. But suddenly the car comes to a screeching halt. *Is there some sort of traffic jam?* you wonder. Again, God assures you not to worry, but you can feel yourself begin to panic after several hours of not being able to see daylight.

Angry, you turn to God and say, "I thought you were going to take me to Yosemite!"

"I was, I am and I will."

"Then why not do it this instant?" you reply in frustration. "You're God—and You said You wanted to take me to Yosemite!"

His answer comes softly, "Actually, I said I wanted *to be with you.*"

Have you ever thought that at last your dreams were about to come true, only to hit a major roadblock? God knows our dreams, our hopes, our talents, our circumstances, our pride and what we aspire to be for Him. In fact, God is the giver of our gifts and talents and often the dreams we cherish. He had a plan in mind when He created us with a purpose for our being. Sadly, we are quick to grab hold of a dream we think will bring meaning to our lives rather than cling to God Himself. God wants us to know Him in a very real way. Again and again He reminds us that purpose is found in the process, not in the end result or in the realization of a particular dream.

If you find yourself swimming in the not-so-big pond of life, waiting to play out the many passions in your heart, allow God to use the pages of this study to speak to you. When we surrender our dreams in exchange for God's purpose and plan, He is able to redeem the pieces of our broken dreams. Such an exchange releases us to trust Him and enables us to practice a lightness of heart that allows us to embrace each day and increase our returns on what He has entrusted to us. Through this process, we will be able to step out in faith and sing His praise.

FOCUS ON THE FAMILY'S WOMEN'S MINISTRY SERIES

And this is my prayer: that your love may abound more and more in knowledge and depth of insight, so that you may be able to discern what is best and may be pure and blameless until the day of Christ, filled with the fruit of righteousness that comes through Jesus Christ—to the glory and praise of God.

PHILIPPIANS 1:9-11

The goal of this series is to help women identify who they are, based on their unique nature and in the light of God's Word. We hope that each woman who is touched by this series will understand her heavenly Father's unfathomable love for her and that her life has a divine purpose and value. This series also has a secondary goal: that as women pursue their relationship with God, they will also understand the importance of building relationships with other women to enrich their own lives and grow personally, as well as to help others understand their God-given worth and purpose.

Session Overview

Women of Purpose can be used in a variety of situations, including small-group Bible studies, Sunday School classes or mentoring relationships. An individual can also use this book as an at-home study tool.

Each session contains four main components.

Everyday Woman

This section introduces the topic for the session by giving you a personal glimpse into the life of an ordinary woman—someone you can relate to—and it asks probing questions to help you focus on the theme of the session.

Eternal Wisdom

This is the Bible study portion in which you will read Scripture and answer questions to help discover lasting truths from God's Word.

Enduring Hope

This section provides questions and commentary that encourage you to place your hope in God's plan.

Everyday Life

This is a time to reflect on ways that the Lord is calling you to change, suggesting steps you can take to get there. It is also a time for the whole group to pray and encourage one another.

Journaling

We encourage you to keep a journal while you are working through this study. A personal journal chronicles your spiritual journey, recording prayers, thoughts and events along the way. Reviewing past journal entries is a faith-building exercise that allows you to see how God has worked in your life—by resolving a situation, changing an attitude, answering your prayers or helping you grow more like Christ.

Leader's Discussion Guide

A leader's discussion guide is included at the end of this book to help leaders encourage participation, lead discussions and develop relationships.

There are additional helps for leading small groups or for mentoring relationships in *The Focus on the Family Women's Ministry Guide*.

UNEXPECTED
Detours
SURRENDERING OUR DREAMS

You shall have no other gods before me. . . . For I, the LORD your God, am a jealous God.

EXODUS 20:3,5

We have desires in our hearts that are core to who and what we are; they are
almost mythic in their meaning, waking in us something transcendent and eternal.
But we can be mistaken about how those desires will be lived out. The way in which
God fulfills a desire may be different from what first awakened it.

JOHN ELDREDGE, *Wild at Heart*

EVERYDAY WOMAN

Mia had a special gift of music. When she sang a church solo at four years of age, all the church members began calling her their "little star." By the time she reached college, she was touring up and down the West Coast, and she spent a good part of her twenties in Hollywood, following dead-end leads. To make ends meet, she began a career teaching voice and piano lessons. She slowly began to wonder if that was all she would ever do with her gift of music.

Mia eventually got married and settled into life with children and a job completely unrelated to music. She still had a genuine desire and love for music, and though she enjoyed singing in the church choir, part of her heart—as difficult as it was to admit—wanted to prove her critics wrong. She wanted them to see that she did have the makings of a star. Now approaching her mid-thirties, time seemed to be running out. At times she wondered if it had all been in vain. *God, why have You given me this dream, this gift, this desire and not let me fulfill it? I don't feel as though I am living for what I was created to do. Is there something more? Is this it?*[1]

We all have expectations for our lives. Each of us harbors dreams and hopes in our hearts that we hope will define our lives. Dreams and hopes offer us a sense of purpose and meaning.

1. What dreams have you held in your heart? To which dreams do you still hold?

    How have your dreams changed over the years? What has caused them to change?

    Can you relate to Mia's confusion? Perhaps the circumstances of your life don't seem to fit with your God-given gifts or dreams. Or maybe all of your dreams have come true, and yet you still find yourself wondering, *Is this it?* We easily fall into thinking that once we accomplish certain hopes and dreams, we will finally feel fulfilled.

ETERNAL WISDOM

Purpose is "something set up as an object or end to be attained: intention."[2] Let's see what the Bible has to say about God's intentions for our lives and compare them with our own.

God's Intentions

Isaiah 14:24,26-27 assures us that God has a plan for the whole world and that no one can thwart His purposes. Verse 24 reads, "The LORD Almighty has sworn, 'Surely, as I have planned, so it will be, and as I have purposed, so it will stand.'" But what are God's plans and purposes?

2. Read Ephesians 1:9-14. What is God's ultimate plan for the world (vv. 9-10)?

   How do you fit into His plan (vv. 11-14)?

3. To confirm your answer, read Isaiah 43:7. According to this verse, for what ultimate purpose were you created?

The good news is that we fit in to God's plans. Just as a parent takes great delight in his or her child, God wants us and has created us for His great pleasure. He intends for us to be a part of His family. This is incredible news for those of us who have endured abandonment, rejection or failure. We are wanted—we belong! And God has a purpose for us in His kingdom.

Our Intentions

Somewhere along the way, we tend to decide that God's purpose for us is not enough, and we begin to make plans of our own. While planning ahead is not wrong, we must make certain our plans do not go against God's perfect will for our lives.

4. What desires and intentions do you have for your life?

5. What does Proverbs 16:9 say about the plans we make in our hearts?

6. According to Romans 9:20-21, why should God have the power to determine our steps?

Like Mia, our Everyday Woman, God has given each of us gifts, hopes, dreams, desires and the ability to plan. But as we have learned, He reserves the right to determine whether or not our plans will come to fruition.

One of the greatest challenges we face as Christians is to make a subtle, but substantial, shift in our thinking—a shift that completely flies in the face of modern culture: *We were made for God's purposes; God was not created for our purposes*. Our human nature tempts us to make everything about us, but ultimately life does not revolve around us at all. God's ultimate plan is to see every knee bow before Him and to hear every tongue confess His name (see Romans 14:11).

ENDURING HOPE

If life is not about us, then what do we do with our heart's deepest longings? Should we not dare to dream at all? Does God not care about our hopes and fears? To find answers to these questions and others, let's take a look at the life of Joseph to gain insight into God's heart. You can find the full story in Genesis 37; 39—50, but in the interest of time, here is an overview.

Joseph was the eleventh of twelve sons born to Jacob. He was the first-born son of his mother, Rachel—Jacob's favorite wife. His mother adored

Joseph and his father favored him over all of his other sons. As a result, Joseph's half brothers were jealous of him and excluded him from their activities. When Joseph became a teenager, he had two dreams that indicated he would rule over his brothers one day. Naturally, this infuriated them. They plotted to kill Joseph but at the last minute instead sold him into slavery; they then told Jacob that wild animals had killed Joseph. In spite of losing everything that had been dear to him, Joseph served his Egyptian master, Potipher, with integrity and was soon put in charge of Potipher's household. Just as circumstances were starting to look up for Joseph, he was placed in prison after Potipher's wife falsely accused Joseph of sexually harassing her. While he was in prison, God gave Joseph the ability to interpret dreams. Eventually he was called before Pharaoh to interpret Pharaoh's dreams. As a result of his encounter with Pharaoh, Joseph became Pharaoh's right-hand man. Thirteen years later, his brothers visited Egypt and discovered that Joseph's childhood dreams had indeed become a reality.

7. How do you think Joseph must have felt growing up within the dynamics of his family?

8. Who gave Joseph his dreams? At 17 years of age, how do you think his dreams might have made him feel? What emotions might have filled Joseph as he shared his dreams with his brothers, who clearly despised him?

How might Joseph have felt when he found himself first a slave and then a prisoner? How do you think those circumstances might have affected his confidence in the dreams he had had as a teenager?

9. Read Genesis 39:2-6,20-23. Did Joseph's detour mean that his hopes and dreams were dead? Had God forgotten him?

According to Genesis 40:8 and 41:16, what did Joseph learn about his hopes and dreams? What can you learn from his observations?

10. Consider the contrast between Joseph's words to his brothers at 17 years old and the comfort he extended to them years after their betrayal (see Genesis 50:19-20). What ultimate lesson had Joseph learned about God?

God gave Joseph his dreams, and yet they did not come to pass the way Joseph hoped they would. God allowed Joseph to take several detours to mature Joseph's heart and understanding. Joseph had to learn that life wasn't about him—just as we do. God also had to temper and heal some of Joseph's childhood wounds before Joseph could be trusted with so great a position. Joseph learned that his calling had very little to do with him, and everything to do with God's greater purposes.

EVERYDAY LIFE

Like Joseph, God often takes us through detours that enable us to fulfill His greater purposes. Take several moments to reflect on the journey of your life, and then answer the following questions:

11. Proverbs 13:12 says, "Hope deferred makes the heart sick, but a longing fulfilled is a tree of life." Describe a time your heart has felt sick because of a dream that didn't come true.

Have you ever felt the life-giving joy of having a longing fulfilled? Explain.

12. Consider your present desires in light of Joseph's story and Jeremiah 29:11. Do you believe that God has a plan for you and that it is for your best?

13. Read Isaiah 55:8. What dreams might God want you to release to Him? Are you willing to surrender to His timing and His ways even those dreams and gifts you believe God has given you?

Consider the following quote by Catherine Marshall, from her book *Something More*.

> So long as I was assuming that fullness of life corresponded to what I was striving for, I was actually deifying my own goal. And, "Thou shall have no other Gods before me" had to apply to my personal-desire world. There was nothing for it but to "put away" the most beloved of all idols inscribed, "What I want." The scrapping of a treasure is always painful.[3]

14. Take a few moments to allow God to search your heart. What subconscious motives may be feeding your dreams (e.g., materialism, approval, fame, personal satisfaction, vanity)? Ask God to begin scrapping the treasures to which you hold too tightly, and to heal any part of your heart that is deifying your dreams.

15. What have you learned, or what are you currently learning, from your experiences in the not-so-big pond of life (i.e., contentment, humility, patience)?

Father God, we are so thankful that You are sovereign over this earth. Thank You that Your purposes prevail and that You include us in Your plans. Forgive us, Lord, for holding on to our dreams, our ways and our intentions, so much at times that we make life about us and not about You. Teach us what it means to walk in Your ways. Reveal more and more of Yourself to us. Increase our ability to trust, and heal us from all of our diseases. The power and glory belong to You for all time. Amen.

Notes

1. This story is based on actual events and is used with permission.
2. *Merriam-Webster's Collegiate Dictionary*, 11th ed., s.v. "purpose."
3. Catherine Marshall, *Something More* (New York: Inspirational Press, 1990), pp. 180-181.

God's Call

UNDERSTANDING OUR TRUE PURPOSE

"For I know the plans I have for you," declares the LORD, *"plans to prosper you and not to harm you, plans to give you hope and a future. Then you will call upon me and come and pray to me, and I will listen to you. You will seek me and find me when you seek me with all your heart."*

JEREMIAH 29:11-13

We must get rid of the plague of the spirit of this religious age in which we live. In our Lord's life there was none of the pressure and the rushing of tremendous activity that we regard so highly today, and a disciple is to be like his Master. The central point of the kingdom of Jesus Christ is a personal relationship with Him, not public usefulness to others. . . . As you journey with God, the only thing that He intends to be clear is the way He deals with your soul.

OSWALD CHAMBERS, *MY UTMOST FOR HIS HIGHEST*

EVERYDAY WOMAN

Tara hung up the phone after yet another conversation with someone at church looking for answers that she didn't possess. Rumors had been spreading about the senior pastor at church. Since her husband was the youth pastor, everybody seemed to think that they should know the "truth." The only thing Tara knew was that she was tired of it all and would love to leave the whole thing behind.

There was a time when Tara and her husband were excited to take this position and were filled with a sense of purpose, but lately they fought restlessness.

They felt as if there was something more for them. Perhaps they were merely disillusioned, but it did seem that God was beginning to change their hearts to embrace something new. *Why is God taking so long to show us what we should do next?* Tara asked herself. But behind that question, she felt a deeper pain tug at her heart.

The root of her desire to see the next step in their lives was a realization that her own identity and needs had been forgotten. Somewhere along the way, she had ceased to exist as herself. She was the youth pastor's wife, the children's mother and a competent homemaker, but beneath all the roles she juggled, Tara felt empty. She couldn't help but wonder if this was what it meant to serve God. Was there nothing more? She felt aimless, purposeless. Tara wrestled with her conflicting emotions. *I'm acting as if there isn't anything good about my life. I have been blessed with a wonderful home and family. Isn't this what I always wanted? Still, why doesn't it feel the way I thought it would? There I go again with that negative thinking. Stop it, Tara!* She attributed the negative thoughts to hormones—and noticed a migraine starting to form.[1]

When we finally realize that we were created for God's purposes—not the other way around—we have the equal challenge of recognizing that life is not about getting from point *A* to point *B* so that we can *really* begin to live. We must focus on the process that takes us from point *A* to point *B*, and that process is about knowing God and defining our identity by His. Even if we have been devoted Christians for years or are dedicated to Christian service, we can entirely miss this point, which makes whatever we are doing seem futile. God has, is and always will be about loosening our ties to what we do, drawing us closer to Him.

1. Like Tara, have you ever found yourself restless, looking for the next thing to happen in order to find some sort of meaning for your life?

Consider the patterns in your heart. Do you continually look to the "next thing," hoping it will finally fulfill you? Explain.

ETERNAL WISDOM

Often in our disillusionment and disappointment, we can finally hear God calling out to us. When we have exhausted our resources and ourselves, God can finally get our attention. He then begins to teach us.

In surrendering our dreams and expectations, we often find ourselves confronting the very fears that drove us to worship our "I wants." Our dreams and expectations provide a false security in an unstable world. God wants to show us that He is our only true hope. In the sea of life, our anchor can't be in moving to a new location, finding a new job, starting a new relationship, remodeling our house, indulging in pleasure, or having a baby. None of these hopes are strong enough to keep us securely placed when the waters of life threaten to push us out into the deep.

Think back for a moment on the things that God asked you to release to Him in session one.

2. What do those dreams and expectations represent? (For example, Joseph's dreams would have promised to meet his need for the approval that his brothers did not give him.)

What do you fear would happen if those dreams and expectations never come to pass?

Do you think that the fulfillment of your dreams by themselves can deliver what you truly want and need?

3. Hebrews 6:17-19 tells us that God confirmed the unchanging nature of His purpose with an oath. What does this hope do for our souls (v. 19)?

4. For each of the following Scriptures, record what promise is given to us when we place our hope in God.

    Proverbs 10:28

    Jeremiah 17:7-8

    Titus 1:2

5. Review our memory verse from session one, Exodus 20:3,5. Is there anything in your heart that you desire more than God? What dreams might He be asking you to cut loose from your heart?

6. Read 1 John 2:15. Do you trust in your image, possessions or lifestyle more than you trust in God? What might God desire you to renounce in your life?

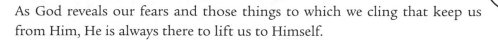

As God reveals our fears and those things to which we cling that keep us from Him, He is always there to lift us to Himself.

7. It is not easy for us to see or admit our own flaws, but according to the following verses, what promises does God make to those who humble themselves before Him?

   Psalm 34:17-18

   Isaiah 57:15

   James 4:8-10

   What do these promises show us about the heart of God? What purpose does God ultimately have for us?

   Let's take a look at the life of Moses to learn more about God's intentions. Exodus 33:11 says, "The LORD would speak to Moses face to face, as a man speaks with his friend."

8. Take a moment to read Exodus 33:12-22. What do you learn?

9. Did Moses have freedom to express himself to the Lord? Can we be fully honest with the Lord in our requests? Why or why not?

10. What did Moses ask of God (v. 13)?

What was God's response (v. 17)?

What does God's response tell you about His heart?

11. In verse 18, Moses asked God what would seem to be an impertinent question. What was God's response (vv. 19-23)?

God and Moses had an intimate relationship. Moses felt comfortable asking God questions we might never dare ask, and God had no problem answering Moses' requests.

12. Keep the relationship between God and Moses in mind as you look up the following Scriptures. Record what each teaches us about God's involvement in our personal dreams.

Psalm 37:4

Psalm 145:19

John 15:7

1 John 5:14-15

EVERYDAY LIFE

We easily fall into thinking that the relationship God and Moses had was unique in history; however, several thousand years later God's heart still beats passionately for each of us, and He longs to reveal Himself in similar ways. He has purposed for us to be with Him, but we must choose to respond.

Both men and women are made in the image of God and carry His likeness. In *Wild at Heart*, John Eldredge examines the heart of women and what our hearts might reveal about God's heart.

> After years of hearing the heart-cry of women, I am convinced beyond a doubt of this: God wants to be loved. He wants to be a priority to someone. How could we have missed this? From cover to cover, from beginning to end, the cry of God's heart is, "Why won't you choose Me?" It is amazing to me how humble, how vulnerable God is on this point: "You will seek me and find me when you seek me with all your heart" (Jeremiah 29:13). In other words, "Look for me, pursue me—I want you to pursue me." Amazing. As Tozer says, "God waits to be wanted."[2]

13. Do you want God? Sure, you know that God loves you, and that He wants you to obey Him, but do you know Him intimately? Can you say that you have a sacred romance with your Creator? Explain your answer.

14. In his book *The Purpose-Driven Life*, Rick Warren says, "Intimate friendship with God is a choice, not an accident. You must intentionally seek it."[3] How can you intentionally seek such a friendship?

Lord Jesus, thank You for coming to offer me life. Don't let me settle into the pursuit of my own dreams and miss the greater adventure and romance of walking with You and knowing You. Lord, I lay my heart's deepest cries before You. I humble myself and acknowledge that I have built monuments to what I want and—in a very real sense—have made idols to help me cope with my fears. You feel the parts of my heart that are lacking, Father. Replace any religiosity within me with a growing, vibrant relationship with You. I want my purpose to be defined by Yours. I want to return Your pursuit, God. Show me more of You and how to love You passionately. Amen.

Notes

1. This story is based on actual events and is used with permission.
2. John Eldredge, *Wild at Heart* (Nashville, TN: Thomas Nelson, 2001), p. 36.
3. Rick Warren, *The Purpose-Driven Life* (Grand Rapids, MI: Zondervan, 2002), p. 33.

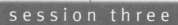
THE MASTER'S *Plan*

LEARNING TO YIELD

Whoever has my commands and obeys them, he is the one who loves me. He who loves me will be loved by my Father, and I too will love him and show myself to him.

JOHN 14:21

We may have the vision of God and a very clear understanding of what God wants, and yet when we start to do it, there comes to us something equivalent to Moses' forty years in the wilderness. It's as if God had ignored the entire thing, and when we are thoroughly discouraged, God comes back and revives His call to us.

OSWALD CHAMBERS, *MY UTMOST FOR HIS HIGHEST*

EVERYDAY WOMAN

Oh, come on! Kirsten honked her horn in angry frustration. The stretch of road on her way to work always seemed to jam up. What should take her seven minutes often took half an hour. This morning she didn't have 30 minutes to spare; she was already running late.

At breakfast, Kirsten's husband, Corey—a wonderful man with a great heart—had needed to talk. Corey was battling feelings of inferiority and depression again. Kirsten had tried to listen and comfort him, but she was battling feelings of disappointment and anger about their circumstances too. Part of her didn't want Corey to stay home with their children full-time; she had certainly never intended to work this long. Neither of them had expected this arrangement to last as long as it had.

When they were pregnant with their first son, Kirsten and Corey had agreed that one of them should be at home with him. They agreed that Corey should leave his job with the nonprofit organization; Kirsten's job made more money, and they knew that God was calling Corey to pastor eventually. But with their second child's first birthday right around the corner, they had expected Corey to have found a great church position by now—then Kirsten would have been able to reduce her workload to part-time. Had they heard God wrong? What was He doing? They only wanted to serve God and bring Him glory; that was their goal, their purpose. Now they found themselves asking, "What if this is it?" Maybe Kirsten would have to stay in her ho-hum job the rest of her life, and Corey would be a stay-at-home dad permanently.[1]

When we catch an inkling of God's plan for us, we can easily try to take over and get the ball rolling in our own strength. Our focus can easily shift from our relationship with God to trying to do His job. Disenchantment then taunts us when we find ourselves in the not-so-big pond of life thinking that God had us marked for the great big sea. We may think that when we accomplish our goals or dreams, then we will know God better and be able to serve or follow Him more fully. But as we have seen, God does not expect us to get to point A, B or C before we start bringing Him glory. He says our purpose is to bring Him glory in all that we do—whether big or small in our eyes.

1. Like Kirsten, have you ever wondered, *What if this is it?* Are you wondering that now? Explain.

What setbacks or detours have you experienced in your life? Equipped with the luxury of hindsight, what advice would you have given yourself while you were in the midst of those circumstances?

We have discovered that we were created for God's purposes, and that our goal is not to arrive at an end result, but rather to glorify God in the process of moving from point to point. Through that process, God reveals His intense desire for us to know Him and want Him.

We love God because He first loved us (see 1 John 4:9), but how can we as mere mortals show love to a holy, immortal God? How does God feel our love?

2. Think of someone special in your life—perhaps a parent, friend or spouse. Do you know what that person likes and dislikes? What makes him or her happy? Angry? Sad? Share a few examples.

How do you demonstrate your love to that person?

Similarly, if we are seriously pursuing our relationship with Jesus, we will want to know how to demonstrate our love to Him. We will be very sensitive to His likes and dislikes and will try our best to demonstrate our love to Him.

3. According to John 14:21 and John 15:9,16-17, how does God feel or receive love from us?

4. Read Hebrews 8:10, and then describe the covenant (promise) the Lord has made with us.

5. According to the following verses, how does God empower us to know His law and His heart?

   Psalm 119:9-16

   John 14:26

   John 15:26

6. That God reveals so much of His heart testifies to the friendship He longs to have with us. How can this friendship with God help you understand your purpose while in less-than-hoped-for situations?

7. Reflect on the following verses. Next to each Scripture, explain what God expects of you during the process in which you find yourself.

   Romans 12:1-2

   Colossians 3:17,23

   1 Peter 4:11

   In light of these verses, what might God be doing in you by allowing you to endure undesirable circumstances?

Take a moment to considering the following words of Catherine Marshall. Fill in the blank with your own dream or expectations.

> Why does God insist on our laying down our wills even when what we are clamoring for also happens to be His will for us? I believe that the answer lies in this direction: . . . God is interested in more than _____; He is intent on our learning how to obey Him in the totality of life.[2]

ENDURING HOPE

Standing at the very top of a mountain is an inspiring and exhilarating experience; however, to get there requires traveling or hiking, which are not always so glorious. We must endure twists and turns—or sweat and sore muscles—and the view on the way is not nearly as spectacular or inspiring as that on the top.

History recounts similar stories of remarkable heroes making the long journey to the top. Reading from a comfortable chair in our living room, their stories inspire us. But when we look closely, we find that even heroes found the long trek to the mountaintop as exhausting and even as confusing as we do.

One such biblical hero was King David. Throughout his life, God made him many promises and revealed David's purpose for His kingdom. In fact, it was through David's family that God promised to bring the Messiah for the people of Israel. But a closer look at David's life reveals that he too had many fears to release, sins to repent and hardships to overcome, and he struggled to follow and trust God's ways. First Chronicles 17 tells of one such struggle.

Once David was crowned king of Israel and had settled into his new role at the palace, he wished to show his gratitude to God by making a temple for Him, where the Ark of the Covenant could rest. Read 1 Chronicles 17:4-10 to hear God's response to David's desire.

8. Why did God say no to David's request? What was David's God-given purpose (v. 7)?

What did God promise David instead (vv. 10-14)?

9. How would you describe the relationship between David and God? If you were David, and God made you such a significant promise, do you think you would be able to obey God forever?

Indeed David and God were friends, and God made His purpose for David's life clear. David's purpose was to shepherd God's sheep. He was to fight off Israel's enemies and create a place where God's children could dwell in safety. David should have had no problem obeying God, right? Wrong. For a while, all went well, but then David took matters into his own hands. David felt that he needed to fulfill his purpose *his* way. He clearly began to trust in his own strengths and gifts, and ordered a census to be taken of all the fighting men available in Israel. In that act, he showed that he trusted in his own resources rather than in God.

10. According to 1 Chronicles 21:1, why did David take the census?

How might Satan have incited David?

How might Satan tempt you to trust in your own gifts and abilities when it seems God's plan for your life is taking too long to commence?

11. Read 1 Chronicles 21:7-30. What was the result of David's sin (v. 14)?

12. What was David's response to this punishment (v. 17)?

By taking matters into his own hands rather than relying on the Lord, what happened to the sheep—David's God-given purpose?

13. God's grace is always ready to embrace us. What acts of grace took place at the altar David built to ask forgiveness for his sins (vv. 26-27; 22:1)?

EVERYDAY LIFE

Although we enjoy a personal relationship with God, we must also remember that we are not His equals. He alone is God. Only by His grace does He allow us to fit in to His plan of bringing about His kingdom. Hebrews 12:28-29 says, "since we are receiving a kingdom that cannot be shaken, let us be thankful, and so worship God acceptably with reverence and awe, for our 'God is a consuming fire.'"

14. Read Hebrews 12:7-13. What does God do to those He loves?

Discipline (n.)—training that corrects, molds, or perfects . . . character.[3]

15. Why does God discipline us (vv. 10-11)?

16. Think about a time when circumstances did not go according to your plan. What did God teach you during that time?

If you are presently in such a situation, can you see any signs of what God might be teaching you?

Read the following words as if the Lord were speaking to you. Fill in the blank with what applies to your life.

I have shown you your purpose as I did My servant David. I have spoken My promise to you and your family. Would you now try to make that which belongs to the Lord yours? Would you rely on human strength and logic, and forget the Lord, your Maker? Would you have Me discipline you as I did David, possibly hurting what I have entrusted to your care? Then wait for My timing and My ways. My purposes will prevail. Learn from David; do not allow Satan to incite you to fight against My will. Your greatness does not lie in _____, but in Me.

Notes

1. This is a compilation of several stories. Any resemblance to an actual situation is purely coincidental.

2. Catherine Marshall, *Something More* (New York: Inspirational Press, 1990), p. 180.

3. *Merriam-Webster's Collegiate Dictionary*, 11th ed., s.v. "discipline."

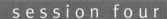

BROKEN
Dreams
WAITING FOR GOD'S PROMISED BLESSINGS

I will refine them like silver and test them like gold. They will call on my name and I will answer them; I will say, "They are my people," and they will say, "The LORD is our God."
ZECHARIAH 13:9

There is nothing—no circumstance, no trouble, no testing—that can ever touch me until, first of all, it has gone past God and Christ, right through to me. If it has come that far, it has come with a great purpose, which I may not understand at the moment. But as I refuse to become panicky, as I lift up my eyes to Him and accept it as coming from the throne of God, for some great purpose of blessing to my own heart, no sorrow will ever disturb me, no trial will ever disarm me, no circumstance will cause me to fret, for I shall rest in the joy of what my Lord is. That is the rest of victory!
ALAN REDPATH, VICTORIOUS CHRISTIAN LIVING

EVERYDAY WOMAN

"I'm sorry, but the baby's heart has stopped beating," the doctor said. Rebecca was stunned. When she and her husband had started infertility treatments, she knew that things might not work out. But when the pregnancy test came back positive, she allowed herself to hope wholeheartedly. The possibility of having a miscarriage after carrying the baby three months had never occurred to her. Suddenly, it seemed her whole world came crashing down around her.

Her dreams of being a mother lay broken at her feet.

Rebecca didn't know what to think. Could they try again? *Should* they? None of her friends had ever had a problem getting pregnant or carrying a child to full-term. Some even had unplanned pregnancies. She wondered if something was wrong with her.

Rebecca felt defective, like something in her had been made wrong; she feared she would never be like other women. Did she even dare to dream about the possibility of being a mother? Had she somehow angered God, that He would keep the one thing she wanted from her? Why would He allow her to have such a strong desire and not fulfill it? She felt she had so many questions, yet so little hope—and life felt strangely meaningless.[1]

Do you remember the 70s show called *Laverne and Shirley*? Laverne and Shirley were friends and roommates who worked at a Milwaukee Brewery. They manned the conveyor belts, making sure all the bottles were aligned for the machine to pick up for packing. The show was quite progressive in its day; it featured two single women pursuing their dreams. Can you hear the lyrics of the opening song? "And we'll do it our way, yes our way. Make all our dreams come true."[2]

How many of us go through life as if "Making Our Dreams Come True" is our theme song? We work hard to line all of our ducks in a row in order to make our dreams come true. But every now and then a duck refuses to line up; a "bottle" gets knocked over and causes a chain reaction that messes up our plan. Who expects the death of a child, an unfaithful spouse, infertility, betrayal, a church split or bankruptcy? None of us plans or invites chaos, and yet chaos finds us all at some point. Where is God when chaos arrives? Is He punishing us for something we've done, or might He be doing something else?

1. Like Laverne and Shirley, do you embrace the philosophy that you are responsible for making your own dreams come true?

Have you ever had to pick up the broken pieces of a personal dream?

What did that experience do to your confidence in your ability to make your dreams come true?

ETERNAL WISDOM

Job was a man who had done everything right. Above all, Job feared and honored God. Under God's hand, Job had gone about his life, building his dreams. He had 10 wonderful children, great wealth and perfect health. Then, as if in a nightmare, Job lost virtually everything. In one day, all of his children and wealth were gone. Within a few days of that tragedy, Job's health was struck. His body wracked with boils, Job was miserable. His wife lashed out at Job in her grief and disappointment, and his friends were better at offering advice than consolation. Job could find no comfort; every area of his life was devastated. Chaos had indeed come to town.

2. Read Job 1:1. What kind of man was Job? Did his lifestyle deserve some sort of punishment from God?

   The unfortunate events in Job's life were not due to his behavior. Read the accounts in Job 1:6-12 and 2:1-7 to find out what was happening behind the scenes.

3. Who appeared with the angels before God in heaven (1:6; 2:1)?

   Where had he been (1:7; 2:2)?

   According to 1 Peter 5:8, why does he do this?

4. How did God view Job (1:8; 2:3)?

5. Of what truth did Satan—the father of lies—remind God in Job 1:9-10?

6. Colossians 3:3 says that our lives are hidden with Christ in God. That is a double hedge of protection! If we stay within God's protective hedge, can anything touch us without His permission?

7. God granted Satan permission to harm Job. What was Job's response both times (1:20-22; 2:10)?

    How did Job's wife play right into Satan's hands (2:9)?

When bad things happen in our lives, how do we respond? Most of us can probably best relate to Job's wife's response. In our pain, we do exactly what Satan wants us to do: We curse God—and then turn on anything and anyone in our way! We so badly want to blame something or someone for our pain. But Job's response was different, and God was pleased with his response. Let's take a closer look at what allowed Job to respond to his pain and disappointment in such a godly way.

8. Look again at Job 1:20-22. How did Job respond to the tragedies that struck him?

    Was Job in denial? Did he allow himself to feel and acknowledge his pain (2:13)?

9. Clearly Job's form of worship didn't include upbeat songs! How does Psalm 50:14-15,23 describe the kind of worship Job offered?

    What does God promise to do when we offer Him sacrifices of thanksgiving (vv. 15,23)?

ENDURING HOPE

At first glance, we see little hope for Job. He appears to be a pawn in a showdown between God and Satan. If that were the case, we would have little hope indeed! But a closer look reveals something greater.

Clearly, Satan wanted to destroy Job. It galled him to see a man with such unwavering trust in his enemy. But why would God have allowed Satan to have his way? Read Luke 22:31-32 to find the answer.

10. If a cup of flour were sifted randomly in the wind, what would happen to the flour? If a cup of flour were sifted into a bowl, sheltered from wind, what would be the result?

Do you think God allows us to be sifted into the wind? Why or why not?

Notice that Jesus did not reply, "I have prayed for you, Simon, that God will not allow you to be sifted." Instead Jesus prayed that Simon Peter's faith would not fail *amidst* the trial.

11. Considering Jesus' words to Simon Peter and in light of our memory verse, Zechariah 13:9, why do you think God allows Satan to sift us? What are His intentions in letting us be tested?

12. Read Job 42. What was the end result of Job's testing (vv. 5,10)?

Was God faithful to the promises He spoke in Psalm 50:15,23? Explain.

Just like in the lives of Job and Joseph, God uses for our good what Satan would use to destroy us.

13. Think of a time when chaos visited your life. How did the enemy attempt to sift your heart, mind or soul in the wind? What specific means did he use?

How did you respond to his attempts? Did you blame yourself, someone else or even God, or did your faith hold fast?

14. According to Psalm 107:22 and Hebrews 13:15, what response does God love?

Will you offer such a response now, even if for a past event? If you still cannot, what keeps your heart from offering the response God desires?

15. Read Zephaniah 3:20. What does God promise to do for those who have been scattered?

16. What promises and hope does God give us concerning hardships in Romans 8:26-30?

Certainly God reveals Himself to us in ways we might not have known had some of our dreams not been broken, but what further purposes might God have for allowing our hopes to be dashed?

17. What does each of the following verses reveal about God's purpose in allowing our dreams and hopes to be postponed or to go unrealized?

Luke 22:32

2 Corinthians 1:4

2 Peter 3:18

Lord, lest for You, we could not stand. You see the pieces of our hearts, our fragmented minds and our lost souls. Gather us, Jesus, to Yourself. Restore us to wholeness, that we might offer ourselves fully to You. Take the pain that has been ours, and use it to bring You glory and to comfort others. Intertwine Your heart, mind and soul with ours. Amen.

Notes

1. This is a compilation of several stories. Any resemblance to an actual situation is purely coincidental.
2. Norman Gimbel and Charlie Fox, "Making Our Dreams Come True," quoted at STLyrics. http://www.stlyrics.com/lyrics/televisiontvthemelyrics-50s60s70s/laverneandshirley.htm (accessed March 22, 2005).

DAILY
Blessings
EMBRACING EACH DAY

Let the peace of Christ rule in your hearts, since as members of one
body you were called to peace. And be thankful.

COLOSSIANS 3:15

We look for visions from Heavens and for earth shaking events to see God's power.
Even the fact that we are dejected is proof that we do this. Yet we never realize that
all the time God is at work in our everyday events and in the people around us.
If we will obey, and do the task that He has placed closest to us, we will see Him.
One of the most amazing revelations of God comes to us when we learn that it is
in the everyday things of life that we realize the magnificent deity of Jesus Christ.

OSWALD CHAMBERS, *MY UTMOST FOR HIS HIGHEST*

EVERYDAY WOMAN

Adrienne was exhausted after a long day of seemingly endless chores and runny noses. Dinner was a disaster. Her angry words still echoed in her ears: "I don't care if you don't like it—*eat!*" After fighting to get the children into bed, Adrienne's heart sank as she remembered the dirty dishes, laundry and bills that awaited her attention.

She felt angry. Sometimes it was all just too much! If only her husband were here to help pick up the slack. She immediately felt ashamed for thinking it. After all, he was overseas fighting in the war. Her domestic duties were blissful compared to his present tasks. She had not yet heard from him this week. Her anger now gave way to a mix of fear and loneliness. What if he never made it home and this very long year turned into a very long lifetime?

Adrienne struggled to remember the last time she felt happy and alive. A smile broke on her lips. *Oh yes, last Christmas. . . .* She had taken the kids to the mountains to play in the snow for the day. She and her son, Jason, had gotten into a snowball fight. She had faked being hurt by a snowball he threw and as he came to check on her, she had grabbed him and showered him with kisses and tickles. His squeals of delight brought the other children running, and before she knew it they were all rolling and laughing in the snow. *It's been a long time since they've seen that mother,* Adrienne mused. Guilt overwhelmed her as she thought of each of her children. They were growing up so quickly, and although she was with them daily, she felt as though she had not seen them in months.[1]

Sometimes we live without really living, don't we? It doesn't always take a major blow like divorce, death, infertility, deportation or infidelity to steal our passion and joy. Daily life can overwhelm us with never-ending tasks, and our unreasonable expectations for ourselves, others and our circumstances can keep us from enjoying each moment. When we focus on all the things that threaten to consume us, we fail to see and appreciate what has been given to us. We can be so afraid of the ominous black clouds that we barely acknowledge the promise and beauty of the brilliant rainbow shining against the darkness.

1. What daily tasks or overwhelming life events demand your attention?

How do you deal with those tasks or events and the emotions that come with them?

Imagine a winding cluster of concrete walkways. In the midst of the harsh gray, a tiny purple flower springs through a crack in the cement. We quite easily see the concrete jungle—it dominates the scene. But to discover the little bit of life, pushing its way up in the midst of such opposition, is indeed inspiring.

2. If this scene were a reflection of your life, what would the concrete represent?

What might the flower represent?

3. What do you choose to see on a daily basis? Does the concrete dominate your vision, or do you allow yourself to be inspired by the flower? Explain.

If you tend to focus on the concrete, how might a subtle shift in your focus allow you to embrace each day?

Whether you're still looking for the flower amidst the widespread concrete or are so overwhelmed you can't see anything at all, Jesus wants to open your eyes to the beauty He has placed all around you, just like He did for a blind man from Bethsaida many years ago. Read this inspiring story in Mark 8:22-26.

4. How did the blind man find Jesus (v. 22)?

5. Jesus healed the blind man in an unusual way. What was the very first thing that Jesus did (v. 23)?

   In some ways, we are all blind men. Has Jesus ever led you away from your "village" to restore your sight? Explain. If not, what do you think it might mean for Jesus to lead you away?

6. What was the next unusual thing Jesus did to the blind man's eyes (v. 23)?

   What did He ask the blind man?

   What was the blind man's response (v. 24)?

   How did God respond to the blind man's honesty (v. 25)?

7. Have you ever found yourself telling God, "I can see, but it's so fuzzy!" Have you ever told Him that all you can see is concrete; that the fine details are too hard to see?

   What does the Lord want to do for you (v. 25)?

8. Take a moment to write a personal prayer to the Lord. Ask Him to touch you for a second time—that you might be able to see clearly and, in turn, embrace the beauty in each day.

ENDURING HOPE

First Peter 2:9 says that God calls us out of our blindness, our darkness. He is the One who fully restores our sight.

9. Read 1 Peter 2:9. According to this verse, why does God call us out of darkness?

How should we respond to this good news?

We can purpose to live for today by cultivating peace, joy and thankfulness. We cultivate the soil of our lives by cooperating with the Holy Spirit. When we allow Him to till the soil (often by turning up and over our "I wants"), He is able to plant and nurture in us the new seeds of His true life. When we choose to offer Him our sacrifices of praise and thanksgiving and let peace reign in our hearts, we shift our focus from the ordinary to the extraordinary in our daily lives.

10. Read the following verses. What habits of thinking can we develop that will allow us to cooperate with the work that God is doing in our daily lives?

Philippians 4:4-9

Colossians 3:15-17

1 Thessalonians 5:16-18

James 1:2

EVERYDAY LIFE

> Sit still, my children! Just sit calmly still.
> Nor deem these days, these waiting days as ill!
> The one who loves you best, who plans your way
> Has not forgotten your great need today!
> And, if He waits, it's sure He waits to prove to you,
> His tender child, His heart's deep love.[2]

11. How can developing the mental habits you recorded in question 10 help you to sit still in your great need? How can such habits help you embrace each day?

12. Take a moment to practice one of these habits now by making a list in the space provided of all the things in your life for which you are thankful.

As you pour out this gratefulness, do you feel a peace settling into your heart? Do you sense a shift from seeing the concrete to seeing the flower?

13. As you practice the habits you listed in question 10, record below the inspirations you gain as you go about your daily life.

Open the eyes of our hearts, Lord. We want to see clearly what You would have us see. Help us to see the people in our lives not as trees, but as souls. Let us see and be inspired to embrace each day because of Your beauty all around us. Free us from all of our unreasonable expectations, and empower us to form new habits of thinking that bring glory to You. Amen.

Notes

1. This is a compilation of several stories. Any resemblance to an actual situation is purely coincidental.
2. L. B. Cowman, *Streams in the Desert* (Grand Rapids, MI: Zondervan Publishing, 1997), p. 62.

Our PRESENT Place

INCREASING OUR RETURNS

Whatever you do, work at it with all your heart, as working for the Lord,
not for men, since you know that you will receive an inheritance from the
Lord as a reward. It is the Lord Christ you are serving.

COLOSSIANS 3:23-24

The height of the mountaintop is measured by the dismal drudgery of the valley,
but it is in the valley that we have to live for the glory of God. We see His glory on the
mountain, but we never live for His glory there. It is in the place of humiliation that
we find our true worth to God—that is where our faithfulness is revealed.

OSWALD CHAMBERS, *MY UTMOST FOR HIS HIGHEST*

EVERYDAY WOMAN

Shea didn't know whether to laugh or cry. As the psychiatrist began to explain that her daughter had ADHD, Shea felt a mixture of relief and panic. She felt relieved that there was a reason why her daughter struggled to complete her work, couldn't seem to follow instructions and acted impulsively at times. She was relieved that her daughter's struggles were not a result of poor parenting, which Shea had occasionally suspected through the years.

On the other hand, Shea felt panic. She was overwhelmed by the challenge. Her daughter was her oldest child. Her four-year-old son seemed to show even more of the same traits. And her youngest, at two years old, still needed lots of attention. In an instant, she realized that she would have to learn new ways to relate with and help her children.

Many years earlier, Shea had agreed with her husband, an adult with ADHD, that if any of their children had to deal with the same struggles that he had struggled with as a child, they would homeschool their children, at least for a time.

Now Shea's fear gave way to frustration mixed with a tinge of anger. Why couldn't things be normal? She had been looking forward to next year, when her two oldest children would be in school and her youngest would be in pre-school. She finally would have had some time to herself. Guilt took over. Shea loved her kids and wanted the best for them.

Fatigue eventually won the strange emotional battle that followed the doctor's appointment. As she collapsed into bed that evening, a thought flickered through Shea's mind: *God, You have entrusted these children to me. Give me the strength to do the job well.*[1]

At times, we all fall into the trap of comparing our lives with those of others. Such comparisons are dangerous because God has a unique purpose for each of us. Since our purpose is not to get to a specific place, but rather something we find along the way, we must practice faithfulness in the small things.

We often discount or discard what God has entrusted to us simply because it doesn't fit into what we've planned for ourselves, or because it does not *feel* like we thought it would once we arrived.

1. What challenges do you face that you feel are unique to your life?

How can you make the most of your present challenges?

In Psalm 27:4, David said, "One thing I ask of the LORD, this is what I seek: that I may dwell in the house of the LORD all the days of my life, to gaze upon the beauty of the LORD and to seek him in his temple." Can you relate to the psalmist's cry?

2. Have you ever asked God to reveal more of His favor when life seems dry and ordinary? Take a moment to do so now.

God passionately desires for us to want Him, but we must ask ourselves if we want Him *as He chooses to reveal Himself,* not as we might *expect* Him to show Himself.

3. Read John 7:25-27 and 12:34. Why did the people struggle to recognize Jesus?

As Christians in the twenty-first century with access to the New Testament, we wonder how the Jews could have missed the fact that Jesus was the Messiah. But just think—they had been taught from the time of their youth to *expect* Him. Think of all the hopes, dreams and expectations they must have had of the Messiah and the effect He would have on their lives. Surely He would lift them out of their ordinary and oppressed lives. They had planned it all out; and as a result, they failed to recognize Him. Jesus did come, and He offered them His way, His purpose and His power to live in their present circumstances. He paid mightily for their salvation, but they could not see it because they were blinded by their expectations.

4. Might you be missing the presence of God and the present purpose He has for your life because your circumstances do not look or feel the way you thought they would at this point in life? Explain.

5. On a scale of 1 to 10, how frequently do you compare your lot in life with those of others?

1	2	3	4	5	6	7	8	9	10

Never Compare   Sometimes Compare   Often Compare

6. According to Galatians 6:4-5 and 2 Corinthians 10:12-13, how does God feel about comparisons?

    Reread 2 Corinthians 10:13. To what fields has God presently assigned you (e.g., job, ministry, husband, children)?

    Do you find it easy or difficult to stay within the boundaries of God's plan for you? Why or why not?

ENDURING HOPE

The present assignments God has given us are not to make us miserable, but to allow us the privilege of being part of His greater purpose and plan. He gives each of us gifts and talents to use in circumstances for which He has equipped us, to bring Him greater glory.

Let's take a look at one of Jesus' parables to clarify how we can increase the returns on that to which He has entrusted us. Read Matthew 25:14-30.

7. Did all the servants in the story receive equal amounts of money?

    What did the first and second servants do with their money (vv. 16-17)?

    What did the third servant do with his money? Why (v. 18)?

Verse 19 says that when the master returned from his trip, he commanded the servants to give an account of how they had used his money.

8. How did the master respond to the first two servants? What promise did he give them (vv. 21,23)?

    How did the master respond to the third servant? Why (vv. 26-30)?

9. Jesus likened the scenario He described to the kingdom of heaven. According to 1 Corinthians 4:1-2, who is the Master and who are the servants in real life?

EVERYDAY LIFE

God has given each of us gifts, resources and talents for the unique situations in which He has placed us. It is only natural that He would require us to make the most of what He has given us.

10. Reflect for a moment on the unique ways God has equipped you to glorify Him with your life. Record these blessings in the corresponding categories on the following page.

Human talents

Material resources

Spiritual gifts (see Romans 12:6-8)

Other blessings

11. How can you use these talents, resources, spiritual gifts and other blessings in the midst of your present circumstances to bring glory to God?

The third servant was lazy. In fact, he blamed his laziness on his master, accusing him of being a "hard man" (Matthew 25:24).

12. The following verses reveal the sin in the third servant's heart. Take a moment to examine your own heart in regards to what God has presently entrusted to you. Read each verse, and then answer the corresponding questions.

Luke 6:46-49—Do you find yourself wrestling with laziness? Upon what sort of foundation are you building your life?

Malachi 1:13—Is God pleased to have leftovers (e.g., leftover gifts, time, resources, talents)? In what ways might you be offering God your damaged goods?

Romans 9:20—Do you ever find yourself thinking that you deserve more? Do you wonder why God made you the way He did, or wish your talents, gifts and circumstances were like someone else's?

God doesn't want any of these attitudes to dominate our lives. They prevent us from living life to the full and taking advantage of the opportunities right in front of us every day.

13. Take a few moments to confess areas of your heart in which you struggle with wrong attitudes about your present circumstances. Ask God to clarify His present calling on your life, and to help you see ways you can increase your returns; then listen. Write what you feel He speaks to your heart in the following space:

Note
1. This story is based on actual events and is used with permission.

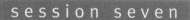
GOD'S
Promises
STEPPING OUT IN FAITH

*Now faith is being sure of what we hope for and certain of what we
do not see. This is what the ancients were commended for.*

HEBREWS 11:1-2

*We step right out with recognition of God in some things, then self-consideration enters our
lives and down we go. If you are truly recognizing your Lord, you have no business being con-
cerned about how and where he engineers your circumstances. . . . Let your actual circumstances be what they may, but keep recognizing Jesus, maintaining complete reliance in Him.*

OSWALD CHAMBERS, *MY UTMOST FOR HIS HIGHEST*

EVERYDAY WOMAN

From an early age, Amy felt God calling her to be a missionary. She had spent
most of her 20s serving the poor in Africa. Although she loved working with
the people, over time she began to feel isolated. Most of the missionaries she
worked with were married. Living in a foreign culture, dealing with a lan-
guage barrier and longing for deep friendship became exhausting. Feeling
she had no choice, Amy returned to the United States and opted to stay at a
center that specialized in restoring exhausted missionaries like her.

"I'm not sure why I can't stop crying," Amy told her counselor. "I
thought I had followed God's calling. I thought I was going to spend my

life making a difference in people's lives. Now I feel like I'm in the middle of nowhere and I have no idea where to go from here. I know I can't return to Africa, but I don't feel like I fit here either. I thought that by coming back, things might change; I thought I would find a sense of true connection with others. But truthfully, I can't say I'm much better off. I still feel lonely and disconnected. Everyone my age seems busy raising their children, maintaining their homes or advancing their careers. I'm almost 40 years old, am not married and know that my chances of ever having children are very slim. I feel disappointed, disconnected and wonder if I haven't been played the fool by God."

We can step out with God, thinking we are heading off toward the purpose He has destined for us, only to find ourselves wandering in no-man's-land. Sometimes this wilderness can seem ridiculous, scary and even counterproductive. In such times, we must ask ourselves if we truly believe in God's promises. By faith, are we willing to follow Him wherever He leads us?

1. Do you feel like you are wandering around in a no-man's-land, devoid of purpose and thoroughly confused?

    In faith, are you willing to follow God wherever He leads, even if the destination is unclear? Why or why not?

ETERNAL WISDOM

Many of us are familiar with the story of Abraham. God gave him a son in his old age and then asked Abraham to sacrifice Isaac on an altar. Try to grasp for a moment the enormous faith and trust Abraham must have had in order to keep believing in God's promises.

2. Read Genesis 12:1-3. What did God ask of Abraham? What promises did God make to him?

Becoming a great nation would necessitate offspring. Read Genesis 11:30 and 12:4. Why would God's promise be hard for Abraham to believe?

3. Has God ever made you a promise that seemed humanly impossible? Are you still waiting to see that promise fulfilled?

How has God asked you to step out with Him, to follow Him?

4. What was Abraham's response to God's direction and promise (12:4-5)?

Have you ever wondered if you heard God wrong? Most of us do! Abraham was no exception. Let's look at three ways Abraham was tempted to discount God's promise.

Test 1: Trust in God's Ability

Perhaps Abraham wondered, *Surely God couldn't have meant that He was planning to do the impossible!* In our natural minds, we are tempted to settle for less than what we originally hoped for because we doubt whether God will do the supernatural for us.

5. Who is the first person mentioned who went with Abraham (12:4)?

   Lot was Abraham's nephew and ward. It would have been only natural for Abraham to think that God would increase his offspring through an extended family member, as Abraham's wife, Sarai, was barren.

6. What happened in Genesis 13:8-9 that must have left Abraham wondering whether he had heard God's promise wrong?

   How did God reaffirm His promise (13:14-17)?

7. Have you ever been tempted to settle for less than what you originally thought God had promised you? Explain.

Test 2: Don't Give In to Fear

Abraham feared he would lose God's promise not only once, but twice. Read Genesis 12:10-20 and 20:1-18.

8. What problem did Abraham face and what was his solution each time (12:11-13; 20:2)?

   What was Abraham's excuse for compromising his wife's position (12:12-13)?

   How might his reasoning have been tied to the promise God had made him?

How did God protect Sarai in spite of her husband's foolishness (12:17-20; 20:3-18)?

9. Have you ever feared a promise God has given you would not be fulfilled because of outside threats? Explain.

Test 3: Let God Do the Work

When things don't seem to be going according to plan, or the plan seems to be taking a little too long to develop, we have a tendency to try to help God.

10. According to Genesis 16:1-2, what did Sarai suggest Abraham do to bring about God's will in their lives? Why did she suggest this?

At this point, how long had Abraham and Sarai been waiting for God to fulfill His promise of offspring (v. 3)?

11. Have you ever tried to come up with an alternate solution when God's promise did not seem naturally possible?

12. According to Genesis 21:8-20 and 25:17-18, what was the result of Sarai's lack of faith? What can you learn from her mistake?

13. Even through Abraham and Sarai's disbelief, God showed incredible grace. Summarize God's words to Abraham in Genesis 17:15-22.

14. Have you ever attempted to help God fulfill His promise to you? What were the results?

ENDURING HOPE

Although Abraham struggled to understand how God would fulfill His promises, he was faithful to obey God in his limited knowledge. He left everything behind and stepped out with God in faith to receive the promises that God had made. He risked being played the fool. What if God had not come through with His promises? What would all the years of wandering as a nomad have meant?

Abraham was eager to see God prove Himself; he knew that offspring would indeed be a miracle from God. No human effort could have established God's purposes.

15. What promise did God fulfill to Abraham and Sarah in Genesis 21:1-6? How old was Abraham? How long, then, had it been since God's initial promise in Genesis 12?

Once the promise was fulfilled, Abraham and Sarah lived happily ever after, right? Not quite—the story doesn't end there. God had one more test for Abraham.

Test 4: Surrender the Fulfilled Promise to God

Consider Abraham's final test in Genesis 22:1-19.

16. Knowing that God's promises were true, how did Abraham respond to God's request? Did he ask questions? Did he follow through?

    How did God respond to Abraham's obedience (vv. 15-18)?

17. Have you ever had to surrender a fulfilled promise back to God? How was God faithful to bless you for your obedience?

18. Read Hebrews 11:8-19. For what actions and attitudes did Paul praise Abraham?

Take a moment to consider your present journey. Can you find comfort and encouragement in God's faithfulness to Abraham?

19. What aspects of God's promises to you seem impossible? Are these obstacles more impossible than what Abraham was up against?

20. According to Hebrews 11:1, what is faith?

How is your faith in God's promises being challenged today? How could you exhibit even greater faith in your journey?

Human faith is never perfect. Even Abraham had a little doubt mixed with his faith, but that did not stop God from blessing him.

21. According to Hebrews 12:2, who will perfect our faith?

Mark 9:17-24 tells the story of a father who brought his demon-possessed son to Jesus to be healed. The man said, "[If] you can do anything, take pity on us and help us" (v. 22). Jesus told the man that everything is possible for those who believe. Overcome with emotion, the father exclaimed, "I do believe; help me overcome my unbelief" (v. 24).

Take a moment to interact with God in the same way. If you are not sure whether He can take your impossible situation and make something good of it, ask Him to help you overcome your unbelief. God honors a heart that steps out in faith.

> *Gracious Father, I know in my heart that all things are possible with You. Forgive me for doubting that You can and will do the impossible in my life. Help me stand firm in Your promises and resist the temptation to take matters into my own hands. I am confident that You will do what You have promised. Amen.*

Note

1. This story is based on actual events and is used with permission.

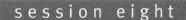

A LIFE OF
Worship
SINGING HIS PRAISE

I waited patiently for the Lord; he turned to me and heard my cry. He put a new song in my mouth, a hymn of praise to our God. Many will see and fear and put their trust in the Lord.

PSALM 40:1,3

You weren't put on earth to be remembered. You were put here to prepare for eternity.

RICK WARREN, *THE PURPOSE-DRIVEN LIFE*

EVERYDAY WOMAN

Thank You, God, that we made it home in time, Beverly prayed as she listened to the doctor. He had just explained that by tomorrow at this time her husband would be having open heart surgery. Beverly and her husband, Ron, did not know how sick he was when they left for London on a theater tour. Now she marveled at God's protection—they would have never known that Ron was so sick had they not been in London and had to walk so much!

Beverly returned home, allowing Ron to get some sleep at the hospital. As she walked into their new home—purchased just a few months prior—Beverly suddenly felt gripped by fear. She and Ron had weathered many storms together. They had experienced many curveballs in the past few years, but this was a new thing. Neither of them had ever been very ill—certainly nothing life threatening. What if he didn't make it through surgery? She would have to live in this house—not quite home yet—without him. What would she do with his businesses? Her work? And how would her three children and five grandchildren respond?

Fatigue hit Beverly like a locomotive. She had walked off the plane only 24 hours ago, and so much had happened since then. Jet-lagged, she fell into bed. She imagined her Savior's arms holding her and cried. Even if her husband lived, the next few months were going to be hard work. She found herself surrendering it all to the One who had held her in the past and who would hold her through what now lay ahead.[1]

Have you ever lost or forgotten the combination to a lock? Though a painstaking process, it is still possible to open the lock if one listens very carefully for the clicks while turning the dial. Initially, listening is quite difficult; but once you know the sound, finding the right combination is a matter of focus. The process of understanding our purpose is a bit like training our ears to hear the click of God's voice, as He whispers the combination that will unlock our hopes and dreams.

A wise person once said, "The faith steps only get bigger the longer we live. I am not sure it ever gets easier to walk through hard things. However, we do have the privilege of knowing how God has worked on our behalf before, and therefore, our faith is greater in knowing that He is planning for our good even now."[2]

1. Does it seem the steps of faith God has required you to take have gotten bigger the longer you have lived life with Him?

    How can the memories of God's faithfulness in the past help carry you through the difficult situations you presently face?

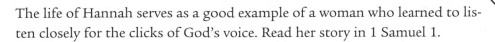

The life of Hannah serves as a good example of a woman who learned to listen closely for the clicks of God's voice. Read her story in 1 Samuel 1.

2. What circumstance was God using to teach Hannah about Him (v. 6)?

3. Can you relate with Hannah—perhaps not to her specific circumstances, but to her emotional turmoil? Are you, or have you ever been, trapped in a situation about which you can do nothing? Have you ever been oppressed by a rival? Explain.

4. What did Hannah do with her pain (vv. 10-11)?

5. How did Eli respond to her at first (vv. 12-14)?

    Have you ever been misunderstood like Hannah? In the space provided, ask the Lord to help you to forgive the person who misunderstood you if you haven't already.

6. Take a moment to allow God to search your heart. Like Eli, have you ever judged someone too quickly? In the space provided, ask the Lord to forgive you.

7. Upon Eli's blessing, why do you think that Hannah's whole disposition changed (v. 18)? (Hint: What did she possess that Abraham also possessed?)

8. We see in verse 19 that the Lord remembered Hannah. Hannah's hope was fulfilled; her faith was rewarded by the birth of a son. What was his name? What did his name mean (v. 20)?

God used painful circumstances to train Hannah to hear the quiet click of His voice. Hannah was overwhelmed with gratefulness for what God had done. He had increased her faith. But the faith steps in her life were about to get bigger when it came time for Hannah to fulfill her vows to the Lord.

Verses 24 to 28 tell the story of Hannah's obedience. Like Abraham, she offered up her fulfilled promise for God's use and glory.

9. Read Hannah's beautiful song recorded in 1 Samuel 2:1-10. Judging from this testimony, how do you think Hannah was able to let Samuel go?

    According to 1 Samuel 2:18-21,26, how was God faithful to Hannah and Samuel?

10. Read 1 Samuel 3:19—4:1. Describe the far-reaching effects of Hannah's trust in the Lord. How was God glorified?

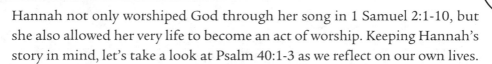

Hannah not only worshiped God through her song in 1 Samuel 2:1-10, but she also allowed her very life to become an act of worship. Keeping Hannah's story in mind, let's take a look at Psalm 40:1-3 as we reflect on our own lives.

> I waited patiently for the LORD; he turned to me and heard my cry (v. 1).

11. How long did Hannah wait for God to answer her prayers (1 Samuel 1:7)?

If you are presently waiting for the Lord to hear your cries, do you find it difficult to wait? How long have you been waiting? Or, think of a time when God answered your cries; how long did you wait before you received an answer?

What would it mean (or has it meant) for the Lord to turn to you and hear your cry?

> He lifted me up out of the slimy pit, out of the mud and the mire;
> he set my feet on a rock and gave me a firm place to stand (v. 2).

12. How did God give Hannah a firm place to stand?

Share a time that God put your feet on solid ground and steadied you as you walked along.

Are you still waiting for God to lift you out of a present pit? What past experiences give you hope that He will be faithful to rescue you again?

He put a new song in my mouth, a hymn of praise to our God. Many will see and fear and put their trust in the LORD (v. 3).

13. Summarize Hannah's "new song" in 1 Samuel 2:1-10. How did her overwhelming praise and trust affect the lives of others? (Review your answer to question 10.)

What new song has God put in your heart? How can you praise Him for what He has done in your life?

How can others benefit from your praise of what God has done, is doing and will do in your life?

14. If you are still waiting in the "year after year" for God's response to your cry, read Psalm 142:7. Write to the Lord your own adaptation of this verse.

EVERYDAY LIFE

When we choose to surrender our dreams to God and enter in to His purpose and will, God begins to make sense of the pain we experience due to our failures, broken dreams and hardships. He empowers us to live for today by enabling us to make the most of what He has entrusted to us.

We find great peace and freedom when we learn that life is ultimately not about us at all. God uses each road down which He takes us, every dream we do or do not realize and every step along the way for His glory. As we yield to God and allow Him to have His way with our lives, we become living sacrifices (see Romans 12:1). Our very lives become acts of worship. We often think of worship as singing a few hymns or choruses, but that is only one type of worship. True worship is adoration, love and admiration. God wants our whole lives to be acts of worship toward Him.

15. How have the circumstances you have walked through caused you to love and admire God more?

How does living with this kind of attitude change your understanding of purpose?

But what can I say?
He has spoken to me, and he himself has done this.
I will walk humbly all my years because of this anguish of my soul.
Lord, by such things men live; and my spirit finds life in them too.
You restored me to health and let me live.
Surely it was for my benefit that I suffered such anguish.
In your love you kept me from the pit of destruction;
you have put all my sins behind your back.

For the grave cannot praise you, death cannot sing your praise;
those who go down to the pit cannot hope for your faithfulness.
The living, the living—they praise you, as I am doing today;
fathers tell their children about your faithfulness.
The LORD will save me, and we will sing with stringed instruments
all the days of our lives in the temple of the LORD.
Isaiah 38:15-20

Notes

1. This story is based on actual events and is used with permission.
2. Quote used with permission. The source requested anonymity.

Women of PURPOSE

General Guidelines

1. Your role as a facilitator is to get women talking and discussing areas in their lives that are hindering them in their spiritual growth and personal identity.

2. Be mindful of the time. There are four sections in each study. Don't spend too much time on one section unless it is obvious that God is working in people's lives at a particular moment.

3. Emphasize that the group meeting is a time to encourage and share with one another. Stress the importance of confidentiality—what is shared stays within the group.

4. Fellowship time is very important in building small-group relationships. Providing beverages and light refreshments either before or after each session will encourage a time of informal fellowship.

5. Encourage journaling as it helps women apply what they are learning and stay focused during personal devotional time.

6. Most women lead very busy lives; respect group members by beginning and ending meetings on time.

7. Always begin and end the meetings with prayer. If your group is small, have the whole group pray together. If it is larger than 10 members, form groups of 2 to 4 to share and pray for one another.

    One suggestion is to assign prayer partners each week. Encourage each group member to complete a Prayer Request Form as she arrives. Members can select a prayer request before leaving the meeting and pray for that person during the week. Or two women can trade prayer requests and then pray for each other at the end of the meeting and throughout the week. Encourage the women to call their prayer partner at least once during the week.

8. Another highly valuable activity is to encourage the women to memorize the key verse each week.

9. Be prepared. Pray for your preparation and for the group members during the week. Don't let one person dominate the discussion. Ask God to help you draw out the quiet ones without putting them on the spot.

10. Enlist the help of other group members to provide refreshments, to greet the women, to lead a discussion group or to call absentees to encourage them, etc. Whatever you can do to involve the women will help bring them back each week.

11. Spend time each meeting worshiping God. This can be done either at the beginning or at the end of the meeting.

How to Use the Material

Suggestions for Group Study

There are many ways that this study can be used in a group situation. The most common way is a small-group Bible study format. However, it can also be used in a women's Sunday School class. However you choose to use it, here are some general guidelines to follow for group study:

- Keep the group small—8 to 12 participants is probably the maximum for effective ministry, relationship building and discussion. If you have a larger group, form smaller groups for the discussion time, selecting a facilitator for each group.
- Ask the women to commit to regular attendance for the eight weeks of the study. Regular attendance is a key to building relationships and trust in a group.
- Whatever is discussed in the group meetings is to be held in strictest confidence among group members only.

Suggestions for Mentoring Relationships

This study also lends itself for use in relationships in which one woman mentors another woman. Women in particular are admonished in Scripture to train other women (see Titus 2:3-5).

- A mentoring relationship could be arranged through a system set up by a church or women's ministry.
- A less formal way to start a mentoring relationship is for a younger woman or new believer to take the initiative and approach an older or more spiritually mature woman who exemplifies the Christlike life and ask to meet with her on a regular basis. Or the reverse might be a more mature woman who approaches a younger woman or new believer to begin a mentoring relationship.
- When asked to mentor, someone might shy away, thinking that she could never do that because her own walk with the Lord is less than perfect. But just as we are commanded to disciple new believers, we must learn to disciple others to strengthen their walk. The Lord has promised to be "with you always" (Matthew 28:20).
- When you agree to mentor another woman, be prepared to learn as much or more than the woman you will mentor. You will both be blessed by the mentoring relationship built on the relationship you have together in the Lord.

There are additional helps for mentoring relationships or leading small groups in *The Focus on the Family Women's Ministry Guide*.

SESSION ONE—
UNEXPECTED DETOURS:
Surrendering Our Dreams

Before the Meeting

The following preparations should be made before each meeting:

1. Gather materials for making name tags (if women do not already know each other and/or if you do not already know everyone's name). Also gather extra pens or pencils and Bibles to loan to anyone who may need them.

2. Make photocopies of the Prayer Request Form (see *The Focus on the*

Family Women's Ministry Guide, chapter 10), or provide 3x5-inch index cards for recording requests.

3. Read through your own answers and mark the questions that you especially want to have the group discuss.
4. Make the necessary preparations for the ice-breaker activity you choose.
5. Have a white board or poster board and the appropriate felt-tip pens available for the teaching time.

Ice Breakers

1. Distribute Prayer Request Forms, or index cards, and ask each woman to at least write down her name, even if she doesn't have a specific prayer request. This way, someone can pray for her during the upcoming week. This can be done each week. Just because we don't have a specific prayer request doesn't mean we don't need prayer!

2. **Option 1**—Provide a stack of magazines. Have the women browse through the pages to find ads that feed their desires to obtain certain goals or dreams. Ask: **What do these advertisements promise? Are the goals obtainable? At what expense? Would obtaining these goals bring a lasting sense of fulfillment or joy?**

   Option 2—Share a personal childhood memory that reveals a child's dream of the future. Invite the women to reminisce about their childhoods. Did any of the women want to be princesses, rock stars, astronauts, etc.? Allow them to share some of their childhood dreams. Then ask each woman to share whether her expectations were met as she grew up.

Discussion

1. **Everyday Woman**—Invite volunteers to share their answers to question 1. Encourage the women to share, but be sensitive to those who do not yet feel comfortable discussing such a sensitive topic.

2. **Eternal Wisdom**—Read Ephesians 1:9-14 as a group, and then discuss question 2. Discuss the implications of being created for God's purposes and not the other way around. Read Proverbs 16:9 as a group, and then discuss question 4.

3. **Enduring Hope**—Although we were created for God's purposes, He still gives us the freedom to dream. Often our deepest longings are from

God Himself. Take a few moments to review the story of Joseph's life, and then discuss questions 7 through 10.

4. **Everyday Life**—Form groups of three or four women each to discuss questions 11 through 15.

5. **Close in Prayer**—Be sensitive to those who might be struggling to surrender their dreams because of the tough circumstances in which they might find themselves. As the women prepare to leave, have each woman exchange her prayer request card with another member of the group and encourage the women to pray diligently for one another during the week.

    Optional: Invite those women who might need prayer or counseling to stay after the meeting.

6. **Encourage Scripture Memory**—One very effective way to strengthen our relationship with God is to memorize His Word. Encourage the women to memorize the week's key verse or a verse from the lesson that was especially helpful for them. Provide an opportunity at each meeting for the women to recite the memory verses. *The Focus on the Family Women's Ministry Guide* contains additional information on encouraging Scripture memorization.

After the Meeting

1. **Evaluate**—Spend time evaluating the meeting's effectiveness (see *The Focus on the Family Women's Ministry Guide*, chapter 10, for an evaluation form).

2. **Encourage**—During the week, try to contact each woman (through phone calls, notes of encouragement, e-mails or instant messages) and welcome her to the study. Make yourself available to answer any questions or concerns the women may have and generally get to know them. If you have a large group, enlist the aid of some of the other women in the group to contact others.

3. **Equip**—Complete the Bible study.

4. **Pray**—Prayerfully prepare for the next meeting, praying for each woman and your own preparation. Discuss with the Lord any apprehension, excitement or anything else that is on your mind regarding the Bible study material or the group members. If you feel inadequate or unprepared, ask for strength and insight. If you feel tired or burdened, ask

for God's light yoke. Whatever it is you need, ask God for it. He will provide!

GOD'S CALL:
Understanding Our True Purpose

Before the Meeting

1. Make the usual preparations as listed on pages 73-74.
2. Make the necessary preparations for the ice-breaker activity.

Ice Breakers

1. As the women arrive, greet them and distribute Prayer Request Forms or index cards. Encourage the women to write down their names, even if they don't have any specific requests this week.
2. Invite a volunteer to lead the other women in reciting the memory verse.
3. Bring some type of children's puzzle (4 to 10 pieces), preferably a three-dimensional puzzle. Select two volunteers for the demonstration. Blindfold one woman and place the puzzle pieces in front of her. Have the second woman sit beside the blindfolded woman and coach her on where to place each puzzle piece. The remaining group members may give their advice. The object is for the blindfolded woman to discern and follow the directions of her guide. The guide knows and sees the overall plan of where the pieces belong. The blindfolded woman's job is to pick up each piece and listen to where it must go. Once all the pieces are in place, discuss the implications of putting the puzzle together as a team. Ask: **How does this illustration parallel our quest for purpose?**

Discussion

1. **Everyday Woman**—Discuss question 1.
2. **Eternal Wisdom**—Life is not about getting from point *A* to point *B*,

but rather about the process of knowing God. Ask: **What stands in the way of our getting to know God better?** Discuss questions 2 and 3. Invite three volunteers to read the verses listed in question 4. Discuss the promise given in each verse.

3. **Enduring Hope**—Read Exodus 33:11. Briefly discuss the relationship between Moses and God. Discuss question 12.

4. **Everyday Life**—Discuss the quote from John Eldredge on page 23 and questions 13 and 14.

5. **Close in Prayer**—Allow a few moments for silent prayer and meditation before closing. Collect the Prayer Request Forms and have each woman select one to pray over during the week.

   Optional: Invite those women who might need prayer or counseling to stay after the meeting.

6. **Encourage Scripture Memory**—Encourage the women to memorize next week's key verse or a verse from the lesson that was especially helpful for them.

After the Meeting

1. **Evaluate.**
2. **Encourage**—Try to contact each woman during the week. If the group is large, enlist the aid of some women in the group to contact others.
3. **Equip.**
4. **Pray.**

SESSION THREE
THE MASTER'S PLAN:
Learning to Yield

Before the Meeting

1. Make the usual preparations as listed on pages 73-74.
2. Gather the necessary materials for the ice-breaker activity you choose.

Ice Breakers

1. Distribute Prayer Request Forms, or index cards, and encourage the women to write their names on the forms even if they don't have any specific requests this week.
2. Invite volunteers to recite the memory verse, or recite it as a group.
3. **Option 1**—Give each woman an index card and instruct her to list five ways that her spouse or close friends make her feel loved and special. Collect the cards and read the answers out loud. Are the answers similar? Ask the women to share what they learned from the answers.

     Option 2—Ask the women to share ways that their spouses and close friends make them feel loved and special, and what things make them feel sad or isolated. Record their answers on a white board or poster board. You may wish to use their answers to launch straight into the Eternal Wisdom section.

Discussion

1. **Everyday Woman**—Discuss question 1 as a group.
2. **Eternal Wisdom**—Share with the women a special relationship that you have. Explain how you learned what to do and say in order to bring blessings into this special person's life. Ask: **How does God know that we love Him?** Discuss questions 4 and 7.
3. **Enduring Hope**—Briefly review the pertinent details of David's story as found in 1 Chronicles 17:4-10 and 21—22:1. Discuss questions 8 and 13.
4. **Everyday Life**—Form groups of three to four women each to discuss question 16.
5. **Close in Prayer**—While still in the small groups, have the women pray for one another. Before the women leave, have them select the Prayer Request Form of a woman for whom they have not yet prayed.

     Optional: Invite those women who might need prayer or counseling to stay after the meeting.
6. **Encourage Scripture Memory**—Encourage the women to memorize next week's key verse or a verse from the lesson that was especially helpful for them.

After the Meeting

1. **Evaluate.**
2. **Encourage.**
3. **Equip.**
4. **Pray.**

SESSION FOUR

BROKEN DREAMS:
Waiting for God's Promised Blessings

Before the Meeting

1. Make the usual preparations as listed on pages 73-74.
2. Gather the necessary materials for the ice-breaker activity.

Ice Breakers

1. Distribute Prayer Request Forms, or index cards, and encourage the women to write their names on the forms even if they don't have any specific requests this week.
2. Invite a volunteer to lead the other women in reciting the memory verse. Allow other volunteers to recite the verses from previous sessions.
3. **Before the meeting,** gather a ½ cup of whole-wheat flour, a sifter and a bowl. Place the flour in the sifter. Ask: **What might happen if I began to sift this flour outside in the wind?** Then begin to sift the flour into the bowl and ask: **What happens to the flour when sifted over a bowl?** When finished, pass around the bowl of refined flour. Have each of the women look at and touch the flour. Ask a volunteer to describe its texture. Discuss: **How might God be using our broken dreams to sift and refine us?**

Discussion

1. **Everyday Woman**—Ask several volunteers to share their answers to

question 1. Be prepared to share your answers to begin the discussion.

2. **Eternal Wisdom**—Summarize the story of Job. Briefly review questions 2 and 3. Read Psalm 50:14-15,23 as a group, and then discuss their answers to question 9.

3. **Enduring Hope**—Read Zechariah 13:9. Ask: **Why does God allow us to be sifted (question 11)?** Briefly discuss question 12.

4. **Everyday Life**—Discuss question 17. Review God's promises as recorded in questions 15 and 16.

5. **Close in Prayer**—Ask a volunteer to close the group in prayer, focusing on being thankful for the promises God has given each of us. Before the women leave, have them select the Prayer Request Form of a woman for whom they have not yet prayed.

   Optional: Invite those women who might need prayer or counseling to stay after the meeting.

6. **Encourage Scripture Memory**—Encourage the women to memorize next week's key verse or a verse from the lesson that was especially helpful for them.

After the Meeting

1. **Evaluate.**
2. **Encourage.**
3. **Equip.**
4. **Pray.**

SESSION FIVE
DAILY BLESSINGS:
Embracing Each Day

Before the Meeting

1. Make the usual preparations as listed on pages 73-74.
2. Prepare the necessary materials for the ice-breaker activity.

Ice Breakers

1. Distribute Prayer Request Forms, or index cards, and encourage the women to write their names on the forms even if they don't have any specific requests this week.

2. Invite a volunteer to lead the other women in reciting the memory verse. Allow other volunteers to recite the verses from previous sessions.

3. Invite each woman to write down on a piece of paper at least three "ordinary" things that she loved as a child (e.g., squishing her toes in the mud, making paper dolls, swinging on a tree swing). Have each woman share her childhood wonders with the group and whether she still finds pleasure in such things. Use this discussion as a springboard into question 1.

Discussion

1. **Everyday Woman**—Invite the women to respond to question 1.

2. **Eternal Wisdom**—Much of being able to embrace each day depends on our focus. Read the description of the concrete and flower on page 42. Invite volunteers to share their answers to questions 2 and 3. Briefly review questions 4 through 7 as a group.

3. **Enduring Hope**—Have a volunteer read 1 Peter 2:9, and then discuss question 9. Read each verse listed in question 10, highlighting each habit of thinking these verses encourage. Ask: **How can we develop attitudes of praise?**

4. **Everyday Life**—Discuss questions 11 and 12. As the women share the things for which they are thankful, record them on a white board or poster board. Ask volunteers to share the inspirations they recorded in question 13.

5. **Close in Prayer**—Form a circle and have each woman pray a brief prayer of thanksgiving. Before the women leave, have them select the Prayer Request Form of a woman for whom they have not yet prayed.

   Optional: Invite those women who might need prayer or counseling to stay after the meeting.

6. **Encourage Scripture Memory**—Encourage the women to memorize next week's key verse or a verse from the lesson that was especially helpful for them.

After the Meeting

1. **Evaluate.**
2. **Encourage.**
3. **Equip.**
4. **Pray.**

OUR PRESENT PLACE:
Increasing Our Returns

Before the Meeting

1. Make the usual preparations as listed on pages 73-74.
2. Prepare the necessary materials for the ice-breaker activity.

Ice Breakers

1. Distribute Prayer Request Forms, or index cards, and encourage the women to write their names on the forms even if they don't have any specific requests this week.
2. Invite a volunteer to lead the other women in reciting the memory verse. Allow other volunteers to recite the verses from previous sessions.
3. **Before the meeting,** gather three pieces of construction paper, two scissors, one glue stick and one felt-tip pen. Ask for three volunteers. Give the first volunteer a piece of construction paper, a scissors, a glue stick and a felt-tip pen. Give the second volunteer a piece of construction paper and a scissors. Give the third volunteer only a piece of construction paper. Instruct the women that you are entrusting to each of them these valuable resources, and that you expect them to make the most of what they have been given.

    Allow the women to work on their projects while you discuss the Everyday Woman and Eternal Wisdom sections. After the group has read Matthew 25:14-30 in the Enduring Hope section, ask each volunteer to share what she learned about making the most of what she had been given.

Discussion

1. **Everyday Woman**—Briefly share your answer to question 1. Allow time for others to express their unique circumstances if they desire to do so.

2. **Eternal Wisdom**—Read Psalm 27:4. Each of us longs for God, but do we recognize and want Him as He chooses to give Himself to us, rather than as we want Him to reveal Himself? Discuss questions 3 and 6.

3. **Enduring Hope**—Have the women take turns reading sections of Matthew 25:14-30. Briefly review questions 7 through 9.

4. **Everyday Life**—Break into groups of two or three women each to discuss questions 10 through 12. If the women can identify with any of the third servant's tendencies, ask them to ponder how they can increase their returns.

5. **Close in Prayer**—Ask a volunteer to close the meeting in prayer. Before the women leave, have them select the Prayer Request Form of a woman for whom they have not yet prayed.

   Optional: Invite those women who might need prayer or counseling to stay after the meeting.

6. **Encourage Scripture Memory**—Encourage the women to memorize next week's key verse or a verse from the lesson that was especially helpful for them.

After the Meeting

1. **Evaluate.**
2. **Encourage.**
3. **Equip.**
4. **Pray.**

GOD'S PROMISES:
Stepping Out in Faith

Before the Meeting

1. Make the usual preparations as listed on pages 73-74.
2. Prepare the necessary materials for the ice-breaker activity.

Ice Breakers

1. Distribute Prayer Request Forms, or index cards, and encourage the women to write their names on the forms even if they don't have any specific requests this week.
2. Invite a volunteer to lead the other women in reciting the memory verse. Allow several volunteers to recite the verses from previous sessions.
3. **Before the meeting,** prepare a small prize, such as a chocolate bar or gift certificate. The prize represents an inviting promise that encourages the women to step out of their comfort zones and risk playing the game.

   Also before the meeting, prepare a list of fun and unique Simon Says commands. The commands should progress in difficulty and absurdity. Invite the women to play, and show them the prize. In a light-hearted manner, read 1 Corinthians 9:24. When the game is over, ask the women to share how such an exercise might actually parallel stepping out in faith with God. Were the women willing to play the fool for the promise? Move from this activity to question 1.

Discussion

1. **Everyday Woman**—Invite the women to share their answers to question 1.
2. **Eternal Wisdom**—Briefly review questions 2 and 3. Invite a few volunteers to respond to question 4. Ask: **In what ways was Abraham tested? Have any of you similarly been tested by God? Under what circumstances?** Discuss questions 7, 9 and 14.

3. **Enduring Hope**—Discuss how God fulfilled His promises to Abraham, as well as the final test of Abraham's faith. Ask: **Why would God persist in testing Abraham, even after He had fulfilled His promise of a son?** Have a volunteer read Hebrews 11:8-19, and then discuss the reasons why Paul praised Abraham.

4. **Everyday Life**—Review questions 20 and 21. Lead a discussion about the imperfect nature of human faith and the processes through which God takes us to grow our faith more and more. Take any remaining time to read and discuss Mark 9:17-24.

5. **Close in Prayer**—Form a circle and have each woman pray a brief prayer asking God to increase each woman's faith. Before the women leave, have them select the Prayer Request Form of a woman for whom they have not yet prayed.

    Optional: Invite those women who might need prayer or counseling to stay after the meeting.

6. **Encourage Scripture Memory**—Encourage the women to memorize next week's key verse or a verse from the lesson that was especially helpful for them.

After the Meeting

1. **Evaluate.**
2. **Encourage.**
3. **Equip.**
4. **Pray.**

SESSION EIGHT
A LIFE OF WORSHIP:
Singing His Praise

Before the Meeting

1. Make the usual preparations as listed on pages 73-74.
2. Prepare the necessary materials for the ice-breaker activity.

3. Make photocopies of the Study Review Form (see *The Focus on the Family Women's Ministry Guide*, chapter 9).

Ice Breakers

1. Distribute Prayer Request Forms, or index cards, and encourage the women to write their names on the forms even if they don't have any specific requests this week.
2. Invite a volunteer to lead the other women in reciting the memory verse. Invite volunteers to recite the verses from all eight sessions. Be prepared with a gift for those who have memorized all eight verses.
3. **Before the meeting,** prayerfully select one to three worship songs to play at the beginning of the meeting. Allow time for personal reflection and prayer. Encourage the women to spend the time privately praising God for what He has done, is doing and will do in their lives. After this time of worship, invite the women to share what God has been doing in their lives throughout this study. If the group is large, break into groups of three to four women each for this time of sharing. Encourage the women to discuss what they have learned about purpose, and how their discoveries fit with living a life of worship.

Discussion

1. **Everyday Woman**—Discuss the importance of recognizing God's provisions for us as we live life. Generally, the steps of faith God requires of us get bigger as we grow older in Him, but our confidence in what God will do on our behalf also increases as we bear witness to His work in our lives over time. Invite the women to share in what ways they have already seen God work on their behalf.
2. **Eternal Wisdom**—God teaches us to hear His voice. Ask: **How did God teach Hannah to hear His voice? How did He act on her behalf? How did God's faithfulness build Hannah's confidence in her future? What ultimate purpose did Hannah's and Samuel's lives serve?**
3. **Enduring Hope**—Ask: **How long did Hannah have to wait for a response from God? How long have you been waiting for God to respond to your call for help? How has God been teaching you**

to hear the clicks of His voice? Ask a few volunteers to share personal examples of how God has put a new song in their mouths.

4. **Everyday Life**—Allow ample time for the women to share their answers to question 15.

5. **Close in Prayer**—Read Isaiah 38:15-20, and then close the meeting in prayer. Before the women leave, have them select the Prayer Request Form of a woman for whom they have not yet prayed. Encourage the women to continue praying for one another until the next Focus on the Family Women's Bible study begins.

    Optional: Invite those women who might need prayer or counseling to stay after the meeting.

After the Meeting

1. **Evaluate**—Distribute the Study Evaluation forms for members to take home with them. Share about the importance of feedback, and ask members to take the time this week to write their review of the group meetings and then return them to you.

2. **Encourage**—Contact each woman during the week to invite her to the next Focus on the Family Women's Series Bible study.

Welcome to the Family!

As you participate in the *Focus on the Family Women's Series*, it is our prayerful hope that God will deepen your understanding of His plan for you and that He will strengthen the women relationships in your congregation and community.

This series is just one of the many helpful, insightful, and encouraging resources produced by Focus on the Family. In fact, that's what Focus on the Family is all about—providing inspiration, information, and biblically based advice to people in all stages of life.

It began in 1977 with the vision of one man, Dr. James Dobson, a licensed psychologist and author of 18 best-selling books on marriage, parenting, and family. Alarmed by the societal, political, and economic pressures that were threatening the existence of the American family, Dr. Dobson founded Focus on the Family with one employee and a once-a-week radio broadcast aired on only 36 stations.

Now an international organization, the ministry is dedicated to preserving Judeo-Christian values and strengthening and encouraging families through the life-changing message of Jesus Christ. Focus ministries reach families worldwide through 10 separate radio broadcasts, two television news features, 13 publications, 18 Web sites, and a steady series of books and award-winning films and videos for people of all ages and interests.

We'd love to hear from you!

For more information about the ministry, or if we can be of help to your family, simply write to Focus on the Family, Colorado Springs, CO 80995 or call (800) A-FAMILY (232-6459). Friends in Canada may write Focus on the Family, PO Box 9800, Stn Terminal, Vancouver, BC V6B 4G3 or call (800) 661-9800. Visit our Web site—www.family.org— to learn more about Focus on the Family or to find out if there is an associate office in your country.